Bilingual Dictionary
English-Chinese

Children's Picture Dictionary

儿童
中英图画字典

By Mei Lan Wang

Children's Bilingual Picture Dictionary For Grades K-3 English - Chinese

儿童 中英双语图画字典 适合幼儿园至三年级

兰儿教育出版

Bilingual Reading Program
Text copyright © 2020 by Mei Lan Wang
All rights reserved.
Published by EduOrchids Inc., Canada

B C D E F G H I J K L M N O P Q R S T U V W X Y Z

apple 苹果

avocado 奶油果

ant 蚂蚁

asparagus 芦笋

apron 围裙

1

abacus　算盘

alphabet　字母

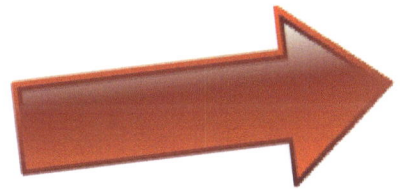

arrow　箭头

axe　斧头

art　艺术

A
B C D E F G H I J K L M N O P Q R S T U V W X Y Z

B

ball 球   block 木块

boy 男孩

box 箱子   book 书

balloon 气球

baby 婴儿

bed 床

banana 香蕉

bike 自行车

cat 猫

carrot 红萝卜

cello 大提琴

computer 电脑

cup 杯子

chair 椅子

cake 蛋糕

cookie 曲奇饼

car 汽车

carpet 地毯

D

door 门

dog 狗

doll 洋娃娃

dice 骰子

desk 书桌

dart 飞镖   daisy 雏菊

dish 饭菜

daffodil 水仙花   donut 甜圈

D

E

egg 鸡蛋

eggplant 茄子

entrance 入口

eleven 十一

Earth 地球

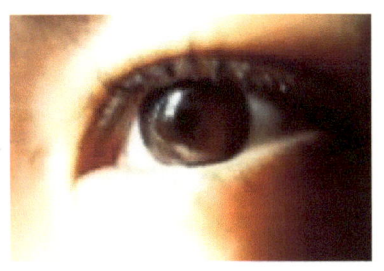

eye 眼睛

eight 八

envelope 信封

edamame 毛豆

eraser 橡皮擦

F

fish 鱼

fork 叉子

flower 花

fruit 水果

fan 风扇

flag 国旗

fence 栅栏

fire 火

foot 脚

finger 手指

F

G

gate 门

grill 烧烤

green 绿色

garbage 垃圾

glove 手套

glasses 眼镜

girl 女孩

globe 地球仪

grass 草地

grape 葡萄

G

H

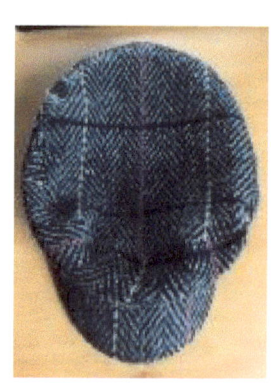

hat 帽子

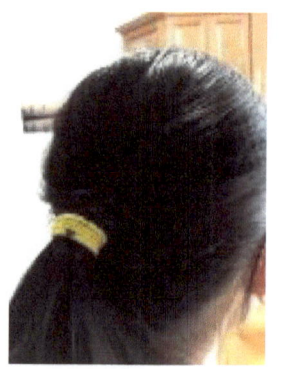

hair 头发

heart 心

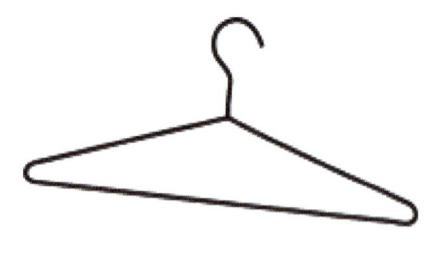

hanger 衣架

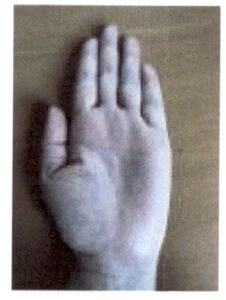

hand 手

hammer 锤子

hook 鱼钩

house 房子

hen 母鸡

hose 水管

H

ice cube 冰块

ice cream 冰淇淋

icicle 冰柱

iron 熨斗

ink 墨水

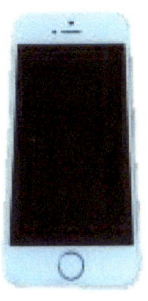 

iPhone 苹果手机   ice-skate 冰鞋

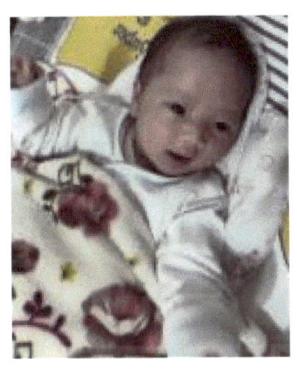

infant 婴儿

internet 互联网   insect 昆虫

J

jam 果酱

juice 果汁

jar 罐子

jelly 果冻

jellyfish 水母

jacket 夹克

jewellery 珠宝

jeans 牛仔裤

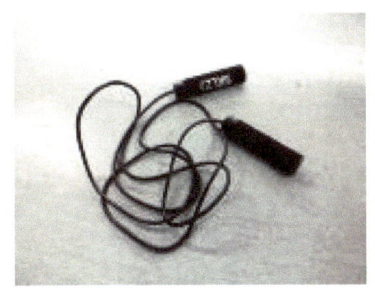

jump rope 跳绳

jeep 吉普车

K

 knife 刀

 kettle 水壶

 kitchen 厨房

 ketchup 番茄酱

 kale 甘蓝菜

kiwi 弥核桃

kite 风筝

keyboard 键盘

kitten 小猫

key 钥匙

lamp 台灯   light 灯光

ladder 梯子

leaf 叶子   log 木头

lemon 柠檬   lettuce 生菜

lobster 龙虾

lotus flower 荷花   lamb 羊

L

M

milk 牛奶

mango 芒果

maple leaf 枫叶

mint 薄荷

mushroom 蘑菇

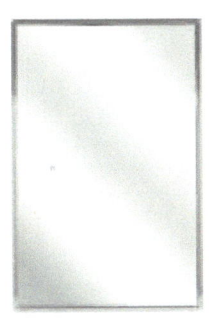

mirror 镜子

money 钱

mat 垫子

mug 带柄的杯子

mop 拖把

M

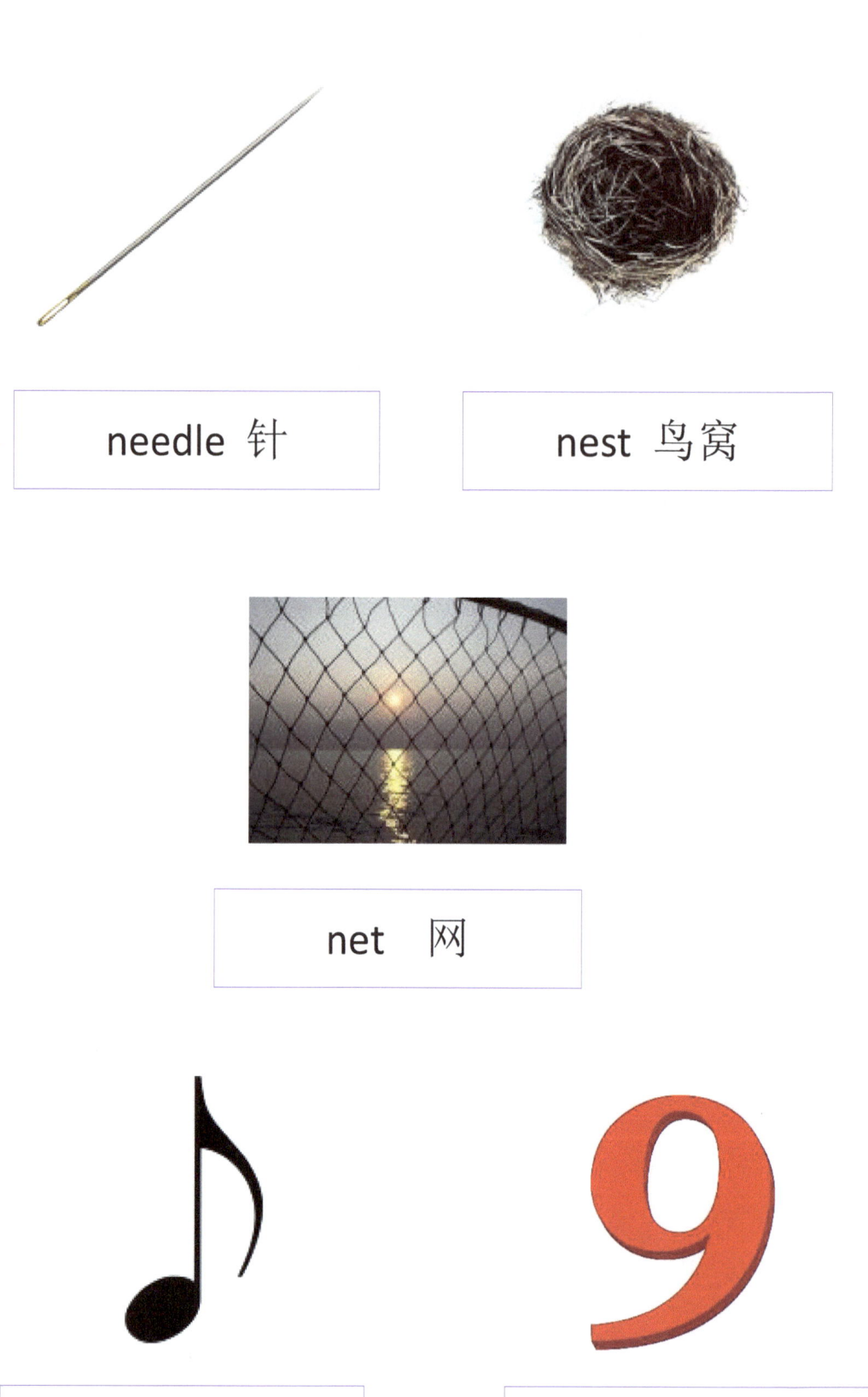

needle 针

nest 鸟窝

net 网

note 音符

nine 九

napkin 纸巾

noodle 面条

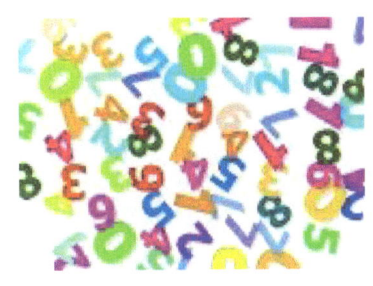
number 数字

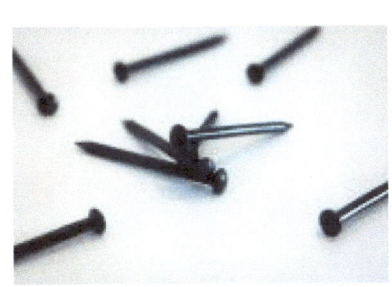
nail 钉子

night 夜晚

N

O

orange 橙

onion 洋葱

oil 油

olive 橄榄

oyster 海蛎

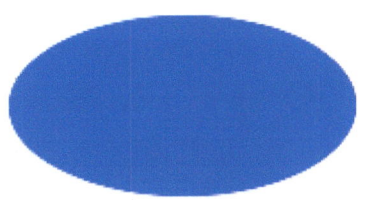

one 一

oval 椭圆

octopus 章鱼

oat 燕麦

oven 烤箱

O

P

pineapple 菠萝

pear 梨

pizza 比萨饼

peanut 花生

peach 桃子

pencil 铅笔   pen 钢笔

piano 钢琴

picture 照片   pedal 脚踏板

P

quail 鹌鹑鸟

quill 鸡毛笔

queen 皇后

quilt 被子

quarter 二十五分

33

question 疑问

quack 鸭子叫

quiz 小测

queue 列队

quartz 石英

ring 戒子

rose 玫瑰

robe 睡袍

R

red 红色

radio 收音机

rice 米饭

rain 雨

road 道路

rake 耙子

rope 绳子

R

sun 太阳

soil 土壤

star 星星

snow 雪

squirrel 松鼠

seven 七

six 六

stone 石头

strawberry 草莓

ship 船舶

T

table 桌子   telephone 电话

tea 茶

tomato 西红柿   ten 十

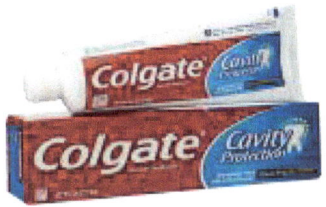 

| toothpaste 牙膏 | toy 玩具 |

tent 帐篷

| tree 树 | toothbrush 牙刷 |

T

unicycle 单轮车

umbrella 雨伞

uniform 制服

underwear 内裤

utensil 厨具

up 向上　　ukulele 尤克里里

underground 地下

urn 瓮　　unhappy 不高兴

violin 小提琴

vase 花瓶

van 商务车

vest 马甲

vacuum 吸尘器

violet 紫色

vegetable 蔬菜

vinegar 醋

video game 电子游戏

village 村庄

water 水 watch 手表

window 窗户

wall 墙 wheel 轮子

wagon 四轮车

weed 杂草

watermelon 西瓜

wood 木板

whistle 哨子

 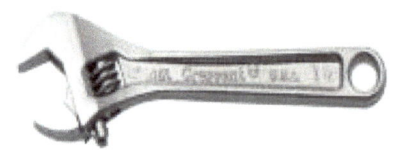

box 盒子   fix 修理

X'mas 圣诞节

 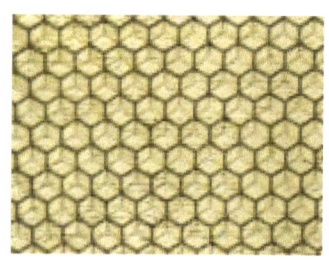

xylophone 木琴   wax 蜡

six 六

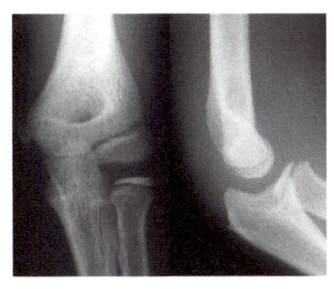

x-ray X-光透视

fox 狐狸

ox 牛

mix 搅拌

yo-yo 悠悠球

yarn 毛线

yard 院子

yacht 快艇

yak 牦牛

yam 地瓜

yellow 黄色

yogurt 酸奶

yolk 蛋黄

yum 好吃

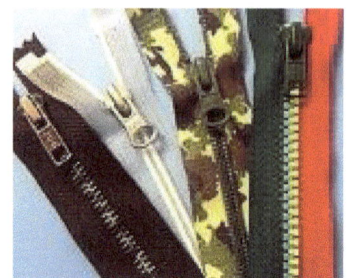

zucchini 意大利瓜

zipper 拉链

zero 零

zoo 动物园

zebra 斑马

zig-zag 之字线

zone 区域

zinc 锌

zamboni 磨冰机

zinnia 百日菊

Index Aa - Dd

Aa
abacus	算盘
alphabet	字母
ant	蚂蚁
apple	苹果
apron	围裙
arrow	箭头
art	艺术
asparagus	芦笋
avocado	奶油果
axe	斧头

Bb
baby	婴儿
ball	球
balloon	气球
banana	香蕉
bed	床
bike	自行车
block	木块
book	书
box	箱子
boy	男孩

Cc
cake	蛋糕
car	汽车
carpet	地毯
carrot	红萝卜
cat	猫
cello	大提琴
chair	椅子
computer	电脑
cookie	曲奇饼
cup	杯子

Dd
daffodil	水仙花
daisy	雏菊
dart	飞镖
desk	书桌
dice	骰子
dish	饭菜
dog	狗
doll	洋娃娃
donut	甜圈
door	门

Index Ee - Hh

Ee	
Earth	地球
edamame	毛豆
egg	鸡蛋
eggplant	茄子
eight	八
eleven	十一
entrance	入口
envelope	信封
eraser	橡皮擦
eye	眼睛

Ff	
fan	风扇
fence	栅栏
finger	手指
fire	火
fish	鱼
flag	国旗
flower	花
foot	脚
fork	叉子
fruit	水果

Gg	
garbage	垃圾
gate	门
girl	女孩
glasses	眼镜
globe	地球仪
glove	手套
grape	葡萄
grass	草地
green	绿色
grill	烧烤

Hh	
hair	头发
hammer	锤子
hand	手
hanger	衣架
hat	帽子
heart	心
hen	母鸡
hook	鱼钩
hose	水管
house	房子

Index Ii - Ll

Ii
ice cream	冰淇淋
ice cube	冰块
ice-skate	冰鞋
icicle	冰柱
infant	婴儿
ink	墨水
insect	昆虫
internet	互联网
iPhone	苹果手机
iron	熨斗

Jj
jacket	夹克
jam	果酱
jar	罐子
jeans	牛仔裤
jeep	吉普车
jelly	果冻
jellyfish	水母
jewellery	珠宝
juice	果汁
jump rope	跳绳

Kk
kale	甘蓝菜
ketchup	番茄酱
kettle	水壶
key	钥匙
keyboard	键盘
kitchen	厨房
kite	风筝
kitten	小猫
kiwi	弥核桃
knife	刀

Ll
ladder	梯子
lamb	羊
lamp	台灯
leaf	叶子
lemon	柠檬
lettuce	生菜
light	灯光
lobster	龙虾
log	木头
lotus flower	荷花

Index Mm - Pp

Mm
mango	芒果
maple leaf	枫叶
mat	垫子
milk	牛奶
mint	薄荷
mirror	镜子
money	钱
mop	拖把
mug	带柄杯子
mushroom	蘑菇

Nn
nail	钉子
napkin	纸巾
needle	针
nest	鸟窝
net	网
night	夜晚
nine	九
noodle	面条
note	音符
number	数字

Oo
oat	燕麦
octopus	章鱼
oil	油
olive	橄榄
one	一
onion	洋葱
orange	橙
oval	椭圆
oven	烤箱
oyster	海蛎

Pp
peach	桃子
peanut	花生
pear	梨
pedal	脚踏板
pen	钢笔
pencil	铅笔
piano	钢琴
picture	照片
pineapple	菠萝
pizza	比萨饼

Index Qq - Tt

Qq	
quack	鸭子叫
quail	鹌鹑鸟
quarter	二十五分
quartz	石英
queen	皇后
question	疑问
queue	列队
quill	鸡毛笔
quilt	被子
quiz	小测

Rr	
radio	收音机
rain	雨
rake	耙子
red	红色
rice	米饭
ring	戒子
road	道路
robe	睡袍
rope	绳子
rose	玫瑰

Ss	
seven	七
ship	船舶
six	六
snow	雪
soil	土壤
squirrel	松鼠
star	星星
stone	石头
strawberry	草莓
sun	太阳

Tt	
table	桌子
tea	茶
telephone	电话
ten	十
tent	帐篷
tomato	西红柿
toothbrush	牙刷
toothpaste	牙膏
toy	玩具
tree	树

Index Uu - Xx

Uu
ukulele	尤克里里
umbrella	雨伞
underground	地下
underwear	内裤
unhappy	不高兴
unicycle	单轮车
uniform	制服
up	向上
urn	瓮
utensil	厨具

Vv
vacuum	吸尘器
van	商务车
vase	花瓶
vegetable	蔬菜
vest	马甲
video game	电子游戏
village	村庄
vinegar	醋
violet	紫色
violin	小提琴

Ww
wagon	四轮车
wall	墙
watch	手表
water	水
watermelon	西瓜
weed	杂草
wheel	轮子
whistle	哨子
window	窗户
wood	木板

Xx
box	盒子
fix	修理
fox	狐狸
mix	搅拌
ox	牛
six	六
wax	蜡
X'mas	圣诞节
x-ray	X-光透视
xylophone	木琴

Index Yy - Zz

Yy	
yacht	快艇
yak	牦牛
yam	地瓜
yard	院子
yarn	毛线
yellow	黄色
yogurt	酸奶
yolk	蛋黄
yo-yo	悠悠球
yum	好吃

Zz	
zamboni	磨冰机
zebra	斑马
zero	零
zig-zag	之字线
zinc	锌
zinnia	百日菊
zipper	拉链
zone	区域
zoo	动物园
zucchini	意大利瓜

This children's picture dictionary contains **260 words and pictures** in both **English and Chinese**.

It's a great reference book for students from **Grades K-3** to learn **English and Chinese**.

这本字典收集了260个中英词汇与配图。

它是本很好的参考书，适合幼儿园到三年级学生学习中英文词汇。

USA$15.99, CAD $21.59

www.ingramcontent.com/pod-product-compliance
Lightning Source LLC
Chambersburg PA
CBHW061358090426
42743CB00002B/53